Literally

Exposed

By Alejandra Betancourt

Literally Exposed

Printed in the United States of America

ISBN-13: 978-0692081129

First Printed, 2018

Alejandra Betancourt

Alejandra.Betancourt1217@gmail.com

Cover Design by, A. Betancourt

For Eddie & Madison, because everything I do is to make you guys proud to have me as your mommy.

For my friends & family for always encouraging me & giving me a lending ear & your honest opinion.

For Michael, the love of my life, for being the love of my life & making my life that much easier to follow my dreams.

<u>CONTENTS</u>

I Turn To You

When things go wrong, I turn to you

Get on my knees and pray to you

When I need to talk, but the ears are missing

I turn to you, I know you'll listen

When words go wrong coming out my mouth

When I mean to speak, but can't help but shout

I thank you Lord for being there

I thank you God for He does care

When I can't talk, you are my voice

When I can't choose, you are my choice

When I am blind and cannot see

What's right or wrong in front of me

I come to you to give me help

When I can't seem to help myself

I thank you Lord for being there
I thank you God for He does care

You are the strength I have within
Know who I am within my skin
You're the only one who understands
The way I live and who I am
With every breath, every strand
And because of you, strong I stand

I thank you Lord for being there
I thank my God for He does care

Can't Stop Now

Happy, sad, kiss me bad

Tender touch of an unpleased man

Up and down with dizziness

Going in circles, what a mess

Side to side tug-of-war

Left lane, right lane, in a speeding car

Can't slow down, can't catch my breath

If do so, reality sets

Must go on, refuse to stop

Full of fear until I pop

Don't look back, can't look ahead

Regretful rest in my made bed

Ear to ear with a stretching smile

Exterior counts with every mile

Can't explode, not quite yet

Too young to remember, they mustn't forget

Mama! Mama! My little ones

Can't go nowhere, not quite done

Sweet "Besitos", loving looks

Big hand, little hand, to their touch I'm hooked

In my life ungrateful bastards

The best reward, my life lived faster

Bumpy roads with no short cuts

No back seat walk was a must

Left foot, right foot, with no shoes on

Last in line and still I won

Happy, sad, up and down

Going in circles with a backward frown

Left lane, right lane, in a speeding car

To my little ones, always a star

Mama! Mama! With sweet, sweet kisses

Makes it all worthwhile, no dirty dishes

Staring A New

I'm shedding my skin
I'm starting a new
Like a snake in the grass
I'm starting with you

Release from the negative
Let go of the old
Relive with some warmness
Away with the cold

Look towards light
Open up my bright eyes
With darkness behind
Along with my cries

What's fixed can't be broken
What's broken will remain

With promises unspoken

The rest will stay same

With what's from your heart

You're not a magician

Nothing will change

When no one is fixing

When you don't take pride

In the treasure inside

When released for your pleasure

More than one time

Reality set the day we two met

With all the highs and lows, I have no regrets

You opened my life as well as my mind

The one whom you love may be the love of all lies

Like a snake in the grass

I now shed my skin

I must go on living

And find love from within

I'm starting with you

Now I find myself stronger

Released from your negativity

I don't want or need longer

One Diamond Tear

I would have walked a million miles away
from you

To stay that way, away from you

And so I did, I found a way

Far away from you to stay

You and I did not mix well

I wore a smile while I lived hell

No longer my husband, no longer your wife

But throughout the mix we forgot one life

He who reflects the image you wear

Tears cry out to have you there

Although I feel the pain I brought

In time it would ease, although I thought

As days turn to nights I thought he'd forget

About the times as a family we spent

"Mommy" he ask "when can daddy come home?

He must be scared to be out there alone"

I've tried to explain the reasons to him

Why mommy and daddy no longer wear their rings

Still every night before he goes to bed

One diamond tear for you he sheds

My Cup Was Full

Drip, drip, drip, drip, drip, drip, drip

My eyes are swollen shut

I'm feeling much better now

Mother Of Mine

I write this here for my dear loving mother

Who always did her best, the reason I love her

Not with just me but with five others

Did it all by herself with no help from a father

We didn't have much, but enough to get by

I remember standing for hours on the welfare line

If that's what it took, that's what she did

And forever I'm grateful for the life that I lived

The world I would give her, that's what she deserves

On hands and feet it is she I will serve

Nobody's perfect, but she is in my eyes

So I give you my thanks dear loving mother of mine

Dear Father

Where were you my whole life?

How could you walk away?

Did you miss me growing up? If so,

Why didn't you stay?

Birthdays, Christmas, holidays

Why'd you never call?

There were times I needed you

And you

You were gone

Did you ever write me a letter

And just never mailed it?

Well, I did several times

Just didn't know where to send it

Do you ever wonder, how did my life turn out?

What I do for a living?

What I'm all about?

Do you think of me?

If it's your image I might share?

Whose eyes I have?

Do I wear your smile?

Do you even care?

You always knew where to find me because
I never left

I always waited by the phone

About me, did you forget?

Did you ever want to see me?

Even just to hold me?

To wrap your arms around me?

To tell me that you're sorry?

My whole life, where were you?

How could you walk away?

How could you never think of me?

Birthdays, Christmas, holidays

To Make Him Proud

When I try my best to succeed in life

But my paths are dark I see no light

I'm doing my best to not give up

If I can't walk, I'll run and jump

When the life I live is not for me

When all I do is for my baby

To make him proud of who I am

To make him see and understand

To help him up when he needs my hand

To raise him right to be a man

When I try my best, but the roads are rough

But I will not quit, will not give up

When the life I live is not for me

And if I don't make it then how can he

I stand strong in all I do

So when he grows up he can too

I'll do my best for my baby

So he can be proud of his mommy

Leave Me Never

At night I hear your footsteps

Walking down the halls

I even start to answer

Thinking I hear your calls

There are times I feel your touch

And I feel I have no choice

I even hear you whisper

In my ears I feel your voice

I can smell your scent

In the air all around

A few times I broke down

From a love letter I found

I'm angry and I'm hurting, I'm screaming
"DON'T LEAVE ME ALONE!"

When everything reminds me of you

In this empty home

There are times I see your face

In the half you left behind

Together we are one

With the other half that's mine

Then I come to realize

We'll always be together

Until the time we meet again

In my heart, you'll leave me never

Me The Poet

My thoughts, my feelings I express in poems

When I'm feeling happy, depressed or alone

And me, a poet, I named myself

When it's done with pleasure and not for wealth

It sets me free to spread my wings

To hear my rhythms, I don't read, I sing

I write my thoughts, it's the way I feel

When I'm in pain, my pen is my pill

My thoughts, my feelings I express in poems

When I can't speak and need to let go

When all I have is my pen and pad

I write my poems it's who I am

I scribble my soul, I empty my cup

I let it all out when I want to erupt

It sets me free to express myself

To be the poet I named myself

Another Page In My Book

I woke up this morning

I didn't sleep much

To the bathroom I went

To give my teeth a brush

I looked in the mirror

I liked what I saw

It was me looking back

I guess that was all

Got dressed, put on make up

Don't need much for my looks

I know I am beauty

Just a little it took

Off to work I go

Walked out with a grin

From head to toe feeling great

And feeling better within

The highway, it's packed

The traffic, it's jammed

I turned to my station

Because I don't give a damn

My tank it's on "E"

The rhythms a flow

The cars up ahead

Their speed is on slow

Relaxed is my mind

Late it's the time

I'm getting docked again

Still all is fine

I woke up this morning

That's all that it took

Another day of my story

Another page in my book

Complain About The Cold

All winter long, complain about the cold

About the view from my window

All I see is dirty snow

Wishing it was spring to feel the breezy air

And when it comes a knocking

I don't even care

Summer is around the corner

And how I pray it comes

Thinking of the shore

And how this year I will have fun

Summer is outside my window

Beaming on my walls

I'm dying from this heat

Oh! How I wish that it was fall

Now the leaves are falling

And the autumn view does show

But there's nothing like the winter

And the lovely snow

I'm Trying X's 2

It's getting harder with you

Each day to breathe

It's been an eternity

But, in you I believed

I'm here with you now

When I really want to leave

Alone I'm with you

Lonely with just me

So many painful events

I can't love you again

Not the same way

Never again like back then

We talked about everything

Together best friends

When I smile, when I laugh

With you, it's pretend

The things you say

I can't pretend they don't bother

The things you have done

My heart they still rattle

Forget! I could never

And it's mind over matter

I feel there are two outs

And I'm the next batter

The pressure, it's on

And it's win or lose

I don't want to live

Life playing the fool

I don't want to miss out

On something that's true

And I don't know if it'll come from you

Or somebody new

I'm trying, I'm trying

I've met you more than half way

Like I said in line one

It's getting harder each day

Secrets We Hold

When I pull in closer, you push me away

When I push away, you want me to stay

When I want to stay, you want me to leave

Trying to understand, all you do is confuse me

Sometimes, the sunshines when outside you see rain

Sometimes, when it rains your bones feel the pain

Sometimes, when it snows we go out to play

Sometimes, when we play it's not always a good day

I heard long ago of a clown who once cried

With a smile on his face, a painter who lied

Of a rainbow outside at the end with no gold

Of secrets we hold and never let go

I'm knocking on your door, you won't let me in

The smile on your face it's painted pretend

I'm trying to understand, all you do is confuse me

Sometimes, when there's sunshine you can still feel a cool breeze

Cheers

I think, what it could be?

A life full of laughter or just misery

I hear a voice, some joy it bring

A sad slow song, along I sing

The beat you bring takes me away

I'm no longer here and it's not today

I'm floating off, I'm in the sky

I can see it all, hear it in your lines

You can run away, you can try to hide

You can fool the world with your skin disguise

But to yourself you must be true

Can't play the fool when you know you

When you can't hide if you are "it"

And if you are "it" why give a shit?

Why play the part with yourself?

Why play a game with your health?

I think of you, who you are

A lonely man in a crowded bar

Across I sit with a glossy stare

As you drink away with the thought, who cares

While you hug your glass with them shaky hands

When you have "no one who understands"

Hello! I'm here right in your face

Can't you see or am I just misplaced?

Can you see what you mean?

You are more than you believe

Let me be your company

I can be the comfort you need

I see myself across from you

At a loss, a bit confused

As you continue to pour your drink

The words you speak, no sense I think

I think of you, what's going on inside?

To feel so lonely, to drown in pride

All Curtains Down

A puppet with strings, I must be your clown
To make you smile, you must put me down

To get your thrills, you must make me cry
To taste my tears, gives you a high

To get you excited, to bring you joy
You must see my person, totally destroyed

Why is it unheard of if I don't lean,
To give me courage, to make me believe?

To see me strong, to see me stand
Makes you unsure, less of a man

I'm not your puppet, you're not my clover
All curtains down this show is over

Iris

Let your pain go one way or another

In a poem, in a song or speak to another

You're hurting inside but nobody knows

You're hiding your pain because of pride

Let go or explode

You have no one to talk to

 So you bottle it up

Afraid no one will listen

Or just won't give a fuck

What's going on in your mind

Inside of your brain?

The thoughts you are thinking

Are making you insane

You think you're alone

And your world is so cold
I've been where you've been
And I know what you know

The pain you are feeling
I've felt it before
In time it will ease
This hurt has a cure

At the end of the rainbow
You must walk the distance
The roads may get rocky
But, this road you must finish

Better Than The Best

I want to be someone

More than who I am

Be a better person

Do the best I can

I don't want what's next in line

Why should I settle for less?

I want to have it all in me

I want to be the best

I want to climb the highest mountains

Then climb them up again

I want to know about everything

From beginning to the end

I want to go to college

And get me a degree

I want to even be asked back

So I can give a speech

I want to have it all and all

Be better than the rest

I want to be remembered

As the one and only best

She's Royalty

I can't believe this

I'm being victimized twice

You did me wrong

And now you want me to apologize!?

I would have done anything for you

I would have given you the world

I put my life on hold for you

To give you your baby girl

For you I did it all

Because to me you were my King

I loved you to the moon and back

Because you were my everything

I still miss you, the way we use to talk

The way you use to listen

I know it's not the same
But it's you my heart's still missing

I don't know how it happened
How our lives just took a turn
I guess it's for the best
You live from life, you learn

For you I would have done it all
Because to me you were a King
I thank you for our past
For making me a Queen

You've given me my princess
And I wouldn't change a thing
Just don't forget she's royalty
And you will always be her King

Five Minutes It Took

This motherhood thing

It's harder than it looks

This lifetime commitment

Five minutes it took

No thought was put into this

No promises made

You thought it would be fun

To lead a parade

Not thinking of me

Not thinking of you

Not thinking of much

Not even the future

You said you would be here

But now you are gone

This motherhood thing

It's starting out wrong

So much to do

So little time

This responsibility made

It's both yours and mine

The baby is hungry

She needs to be fed

No time to sleep

Or just rest my head

Where have you been?

You can't change your mind

It's too late to say

Yourself you must find

You can't run away

You can't say good-bye

She's wearing your face

She can't be denied

Just give her a chance

Some love and some time

This lifetime commitment

It's not only mine

You Haven't A Clue

You think I'm going to stay home

Cry, dwell on the past?

You thought I'd stay hurt

You didn't know I heal fast

Did you think when you left

I'd die because you're gone?

I picked up the pieces

Put them together and moved on

Inside I was dying

And outside it did show

You never bothered to fix it

To allow us to grow

You never bothered to finish

This family we started

You turned your back on us

Left, that's how you parted

If that's what it took

To make you a man

To feel in control

Then I understand

To be like the others

Part time to your daughter

That makes you a man

Or just less of a father?

Me, I'm okay

I know I am strong

And the way I will raise her

She too will move on

We won't dwell on the past

On a runaway father

We won't show love for those

Who with us do not bother

You thought I was weak

You thought I'd stay down!?

You thought I would crumble

And stay on the ground!?

You thought that my world

Revolved around you!?

You think and you thought

But you haven't a clue!

I'm A Ten Not A Nine

You left me now you're back

But I'm not satisfied

You have to come bigger

I'm a ten not a nine

You have forgotten how to treat me

The things I expect

Not selfish, not greedy

Just can't settle for less

I know what I'm worth

And I deserve more

All the pain you once caused

Your return was no cure

How I wish you stayed away

You should have never come back

Don't understand why, to my actions

You still don't react

When I speak, when we talk

To you, it's me whining

Long ago I remember

You treated me like diamonds

Long ago from today

Now I'm not satisfied

You have forgotten who I am

I'm a ten not a nine

One Last Good-Bye

Good-bye to you

When there is nothing left to say

When the way that I feel

To you, I can no longer explain

It's the person you are

You wouldn't understand

My love, trust and honesty

I've given all I have

What else can I say?

What else can I do?

When all that I do

Is never good enough for you

Still, I stand strong

Stand tall on my feet

I won't let anyone put me down
No more insecurities

So farewell, my friend
When there's nothing left to say
Just know from now on
I will lead my own parade

No one else will control me
Like you did in the past
Never again will be put down
Treated like trash

What else can I say?
What else can I do?
When there is nothing left
Just my last good-bye to you

Sober Mind

I hear you calling, I refuse to answer

I smell your presence, but refuse to taste

My face it's sweating, look at me hesitate

Eye to eye we meet, but no more mistakes

You make me weak, you make me strong

You, in my system, do not belong

You are the reason my life went wrong

I lost too much for so long

The things I've done to keep you with me

Destroyed myself, my health and body

I hear your voice, I can't pretend

To not want to see you, feel you again

I refuse to answer that knocking door

From my face, I'm sweating, but no more

Not again will you see me fly on the floor

I refuse to answer, not like before

Try To Cover The Real

Beginning anew - Beginning a bold

Start in the middle - I'm getting too old

Trying to remember - Trying to forget

My mind let it go - My heart just won't let it

Walk the dark streets of flashing red lights

Looking to strangers to look at their frights

Looking back at me they seem to see same

Of tears they once shed, their heartaches, their pain

Live for my future - live for my past

Dwell on the sorrow - or live life to laugh

With a smile on my face - does it cover the real?

The way they smile back - they know the real feel

Trying to remember – Trying to forget

My mind let it go – My heart just won't let it

A Rhythm To Live

A lifetime ago you promised to love me

A lifetime ago you didn't have to promise a thing

I knew how you felt without saying a word

The feelings you felt, I felt them within

With a smile from your face, you'd tell me a story

I loved I just knew, never once had to worry

Never once had to ask, how today you were feeling

If I did you would answer and your words I believed in

A lifetime ago, it still feels like white snow

With a look from your eyes I knew all to know

My days were lived happy, my nights satisfied

This feeling was brought on from the love in your eyes

Let's not forget to mention what your voice did

Your words sound like music with the rhythm to live

From the beat of your voice my body would dance

Hypnotized to your tunes, never once had a chance

With a smile from your face, I knew all was fine

Never doubted a thing with you by my side

Things seem the same, but OH how they've changed

A lifetime ago we didn't share the same name

We didn't wear our gold bands

We didn't share the same bed

We didn't speak much in words

We just knew in our heads

A lifetime ago, still today I'm your Queen

The lines you still speak are like lyrics to me

A lifetime ago, still today you're my King

OH things they have changed but I wouldn't
change a thing

My Life Is Still The Same

Get the whisky from the bar

The glass off of the shelf

Take a breath, pour a drink

Begin hurting myself

Take a shot, then another

And another after that

I see the room start a spinning

Now there's no turning back

Try to walk to the kitchen

But, I can't so I crawl

There's someone trying to stop me

I look up it's the wall

Now I don't know where I'm at

Or even where I'm going

So I go back to the room

Start my drinking and my pouring

I don't know what happened next

But I'm lying in my bed

Tried to get up in the morning

But the pounding in my head

So I asked myself this question

What did my drinking change?

Besides this splitting headache

My life is still the same

I Still Remember

I still remember when I was two

It was me and mom and then came you

I was told to call you dad

You were the father I never had

My mom would go and work till late

With you is whom I'd stay and wait

I still remember when I was five

The way you would touch me all the time

And I remember when I was nine

You went too far, you crossed the line

I never thought it's me you'd hurt

You held me down, you ripped my shirt

You pulled my pants down to my knees

To explain the rest, there is no need

I still remember the thoughts I thought

I should have listened, it's all my fault

That's not true and now I know

I was scared, I was nine years old

Off With My Hat

All I do is write to express how I feel

To have someone sit and listen

To me is so unreal

I don't have anyone to talk to

To allow me to pour out

So when I explode inside

Forgive me if I shout

I don't mean to take it out on you

But you're the reason why

I grab my paper and my pen

Sit to write and cry

You used to be so different

I think you should let me know

What happened to our love?

Why did you let it go?

What did I do that was so wrong

To have it taken away?

We used to be so happy

What happened to those days?

You used to say the sweetest things

Everything I wanted to hear

They were my words just rearranged

Music to my ears

I never thought you'd hurt me

Knowing about my past

To me you were a fairytale

My slipper made of glass

You were my perfect painting

A masterpiece to me

I've never seen an imitation

In a fancy gallery

I honestly believed in you

You found the fool in me

Off with my hat, I bow down to you

For making me believe

Only On The Outside

I'm laughing on the outside

When I really want to cry

And when you see me crying

It's when I really want to die

And when you see me happy

Doesn't mean that's how I feel

And when you see me upset

It's because with life I could no longer deal

When you see me thinking

The thoughts I think are wild

Slash my wrist or pop some pills

But then I think, I have a child

So when you see me smiling

Don't think that all is fine

And when you see me laughing
Just know it's only on the outside

And when you see me thinking
Don't let me think for long
And when you see me laughing
Just know there's something wrong

It Never Occurred

Each day and night I prayed my Lord

To brighten up my paths

To open up my doors

For so very long

My prayers stayed the same

But, the life I was living never changed

Not one time did I see a sign

Was I not looking?

Was it I who was blind?

So many times I got down on my knees

To ask my Lord, come help me please

Never once did it occur

To ask for forgiveness

For the sins in my past

Never once asked for holiness

I never changed my actions

My reckless behavior

Yet I was on my knees

Begging my savior

So now I lay me down to sleep

I ask my Lord to forgive me please

For all my sins in my past

I ask my Lord to make me laugh

To brighten up my paths

Open up my doors

Now you hear me

I thank you Lord

Because Of You

You taught me things I've never known
You showed me things I've never seen
You made me feel like I never felt
You're so unreal, you're like a dream

You touched my soul, you touched my heart
I can't explain or even start
It's the things you do, the things you say
It's the person you are, I can't even explain

You made me proud, I believe in me
My dreams seem closer I can finally reach
Because of you and your beliefs
You made me proud to believe in me

4x's This Week

I thought of you last night

For the fourth time this week

I don't mean to think of you

These thoughts, on me they creep

At first I tried to ignore them

But they continued to arise

With my heavy breathing

Chills shivered down my spine

With my mind at work

Some may label it perversion

I like to think them insecure

With sexual disturbance

Well, anyway, back to my story

And my imagination

I thought of you four times this week

Therapeutic to my tension

I tossed and turned with inspiration

I couldn't control my thoughts

My hands they traveled with masturbation

And other toys I bought

In and out repeatedly

With thoughts I thought of we

Me on top, you below

You running wild in me

I could almost feel you breathing

When I closed my eyes

For a minute I almost thought

You were by my side

With your look, you looked at me

With a look of pure sexuality

The whole time I'm touching me

Wishing you were me

Thoughts of you, thoughts of me

We, soaking in my tub

It felt like heaven when I released

A dozen flying doves

It felt so good I thought you done

With the power to let go

I thought of you four times this week

And every night we both explode

I Am Happy With Me

You always call me names

"The ugly duckling" or "Shamu"

I don't think I'm ugly

I kind of think I'm cute

When I buy new outfits

You ask me, why I bother

The pants are way too tight

The shirt makes me look much fatter

My hair is always messy

My make-up is never right

My eye shadow is too dark

My lipstick it's too light

You never give me compliments

There's always something wrong

My skirt it's a little wrinkled

My hair is way too long

Every time I'm out without you

Everyone looks at me

Like a magnet, I'm magnetic

They all think I'm pretty

They want to buy me dinner

They want to buy me drinks

They want to buy me flowers

They ask me, what I think

So you can think I'm ugly

You can think I'm fat

I think you are jealous

So, what do you think of that!?

Simple Things

Sugar coated candy

A pocket full of dough

Bright blue skies full of clouds

To have someone to hold

Sailing on a boat

With a view of the sea

Blowing wind through my hair

You being there with me

Staying up till late

Talking on the phone

Knowing that you're listening

Not being all alone

The way a baby smells

A single stem red rose

Does not compare to the way I feel

From the scent of your clothes

A warm cup of cocoa

On a cold winter night

Looking at you sleep

The most beautiful sight

The pounding of my heart

Listen to my beat

Coming home frustrated

You listen while I speak

Making me your Queen

Marrying my King

These are simple things

That mean everything to me

High With Pride

I have made more than my share of mistakes
in the past

Forever they'll stick with me, in my life they
will last

So many wrong turns

So many lessons well learned

The titles I've been labeled

So many well earned

I can't take them back

I can't reverse time

I won't hold my head down

My head held up high with pride

There's no need to keep apologizing

When forgiveness you give

So there's nothing left to do

Just my life continue to live

For things I have done

Some I regret

For the good I've accomplished

So many forget

Can't see the good in me

Myself, I have tainted

The masterpieces I've created

Are labeled as "paintings"

Still, my head held high with pride

I have nothing to hide

The life I still live

It's full of colors inside

No need to apologize

For the person I am now

Love me or hate me

I am me and I am proud

A Promise Of My Love

I don't have much to offer

And money I have less

Don't drive a fancy car

To this, I do confess

I could never give you diamonds

Not even a string of pearls

I could never take you shopping

But still you'll have the world

I would never make you cry

Not a tear with me you'll shed

I would never hurt your feelings

All my love you'll have instead

Your life filled up with joy

That's one thing I can give

A promise of my love

And another reason to live

Roller Coaster Mind

If I had a chance to have a wish and wish it
true

My wish would be to have you loving me

The way I'm loving you

To have you take a tour

Around my roller coaster mind

And through all the twist and turns

At the end, like the things you find

To have you take a dive

In the ocean of my soul

Swim through dangerous waters

And never let me go

To know me as a person

As a lover and a friend

To never have regrets

To want to do it all again

I Don't Need

I don't need diamonds

I don't need pearls

As long as I have you

I have the world

I don't need your money

Or the things it may bring

As long as I have you

I have everything

I don't need the cars

The 24 karat gold

I don't need the furs

Or the brand new wardrobe

The riches you have

Do not impress me

So the things that you have

It's one thing I do not need

Release My Pain On You

I have this hate inside of me
From all you put me through
I hold this anger and this pain
To release it out on you

You don't see what you took
And I see you don't care
If you took the time to look
You'll see there's nothing there

I am empty inside me
You're the one I blame
You took everything out of me
My body you have drained

I won't show the world my pain
So this smile I have to fake

When alone, I let loose

This feeling I can't shake

All my pain has turned to hate

I hold this here for you

So you can feel all my hurt

All the pain you put me through

Groupie

The words I speak

Don't always make sense

When they come from the heart

And my heart does not comprehend

Does not understand

Why you treat me the way that you do

Does not understand

Why I can't stop loving you

My eyes do not see

What my mind needs it to see

Afraid of what's there

You do not deserve me

My heart has taken over

It has blinded me to the real

It doesn't want a reason to stop

Feeling what it feels

Don't know what to think

My mind, it's confused

When you have made your choice

And I don't know how to choose

I'm feeling like a groupie

Like your biggest fan

My heart just cares too much

While yours don't give a damn

Don't You Dare Give Up!

When the world turns against you
And life is feeling rough
When you seem to do your best
And even that's not good enough
Don't give up!

When you go above and beyond
And no one even noticed
When you're going a mile a minute
And your focus it's unfocused
Don't you give up!

When your tears come down like rain
When your heart is full of pain
When alone you feel you're standing
When friends and family left you abandoned
Don't you dare give up!

When life is not worth living
Just know in you, I still believe in
And there's nothing you can't do
And you can make it through
Just don't you dare give up!

When there's no one quite like you
That can smile as bright as you
When the world has let you down
Just know I'm still around
And I won't give up on you!

I Am Woman

Let me tell you what I'm all about
With a whisper, no need to shout
I am more than ass and breasts
I am woman, yes, be impressed

I'll lick my lips and wiggle my hips
And now I know the things you think
With my eyes, I'll give a wink
I'll leave you drooling like a sink

I am beauty plus more and smarts
I'll take your job, I'll break your heart
With my heels I'll walk on you
From your head down to your shoes

I am the boss and I am the best
I am woman, yes, be impressed

Johanna's Pride

Johanna's Pain

Mama!

Don't leave, I still need you with me

There's so much to learn

You have so much to teach

Mama!

Don't go I'm feeling confused

I still need you to help me pick and choose

Mama!

Come back don't leave me alone

I'm feeling so cold and I have no one to hold

Mama!

I'm hurting inside, but my eyes they stay dry

I have no emotions

When I've gone numb inside

I'm still a little girl lost in this world

Mama!

I feel like a pebble in a sea full of pearls

Mama, come reach and take me with you

I need to know you have someone too

Mama, come visit when you see my eyes closed

Paint me a picture when the thorn stem had rose

Mama don't leave, help me remember

Don't allow me forget our times spent together

Mama

I'll stay for as long as you let me

But if you promise me, mama, to never forget me

Brother Bear

Brother, father, son and friend was he

A man of pride living confusedly

Temptation took over from time to time

Confessed to his weakness, never denied

A man with a heart as big as the next

The beat of the drums was seen from his chest

The love he held, the love he expressed

When he spoke he would sing his pain to the rest

Fighting his demons was the story he told

Every day was a struggle

Trying not to unfold

Trying to keep it together

Trying to stay on the right track

Trying to do right by God

When darkness attacked

Brother, father, son and friend was he

A man with a heart that was seldom seen

Beauty was his picture and even deeper
within

Exterior with a toughness, with the softest of
skin

With a smile that would shine

And make anyone's day

The sound of his laughter

In my heart it still plays

Forget him, I will never

For he is part of my past

In peace he now rest

Thank God, now at last

Tears will come rolling

But not because you're gone

Because I know you're now happy

Where you finally belong

You no longer will suffer

You're free from your pain

No more storms will come crashing

Safe from the rain

Fly now my brother, son, father and friend

And watch over us until we meet again

Your Only Fan

Wonderland what a scam

The life you're living, it's not so glam

Pretend to be, make believe

Have the world, full of greed

Looking lovely full of perfection

The stories told are your deception

Not so true, full of false

Never thought of what's the cost

Tip tip toe with your stilettoes

Walking tall, so scared to let go

Never knowing of what you're capable

Have no talent, easily disposable

So so cute, so so sad

Have no love, too too bad

Wonderland what a scam

Look at you, your only fan

It Belongs To Me

My heart, it's long gone
You no longer own it
My heart is now strong
With songs of a poet

It sings with the truth
That you could never see
Deaf to your ears
It screams with honesty

Blind to your eyes
You could never hear
The hurt that I held
When the image was clear

You no longer own it
It belongs to me

I'll handle it with care
Like it was meant to be

With songs of a poet
I will let it sing
Set it free, let it be
Let it fly, spread my wings

You no longer own it
And I'm finally at ease
I no longer wonder
If you are being pleased

It's no longer weak
My heart is now strong
It's no longer lost
It's safe where it belongs

Please!

Don't flatter yourself please!

You ain't worth the tears I've cried

Nor the blood I bleed

You ain't worth the hurt I feel

All the pain you've caused me

The image I've reflected on your behalf

You ain't worth it all, not even half

Look at me, to some a Queen

The perfect spouse in me they see

Some confused why I stayed with you

I must admit I wondered too

Tried to see the person in me

Wish for you to be, or try at least

To give what I gave, feel what I felt

To have you look at me

91

Have your heart melt

From day one I knew inside

The words you spoke were all lies

But needy me, needed you

Or anyone to love me too

Don't flatter yourself

 It could have been anyone

Who pretended to love me

Or enjoyed my fun

Because look at me

Look at you

I stand a TEN and you, a -2

A package complete there is in me

And empty you will never equal me

Hooked

I'm so addicted to you

I know I need some help

I can't seem to live with you

And to live without you is hell

Every time in every fight

I swear this is it

Please get out!

Don't come back!

I'm so tired of your shit!

So now you're gone

It's been a week

I wonder if you'll come back

The phone rings, it is you

Then here I go with my act

"What do you want!?

Why are you calling!?

Is there something that you need!?"

And with that voice you sound so sweet

You just called to talk to me

For four days it feels so good

Just like a honeymoon

Then here we go, not again!

It happens way too soon

"I'm so tired of your shit!

You're never going to change!

Walk away, leave me alone!

Why don't you act your age!?"

Like A Volcano

Your tongue so wet

As you lick my inner thighs

You got me going crazy

Wild thoughts run through my mind

The sound of you breathing

The warmth of your breath

One hand on my hips

The other on my breast

The feeling you give

I swear I can't take it

I'm going to explode

Through the night I won't make it

My legs wrapped around you

You pulling me closer

I'm holding on tight

Your hands on my shoulders

I'm getting much hotter

I'm dripping with sweat

The sheets on the bed

They are all soaked and wet

I love how you love me

When my body you hold

The sound of your voice

When you're about to explode

I love how you taste

When your flavor I lick

And I love how you feel

When you're as hard as a brick

I swear I can't take it

I'm about to explode

I'm about to erupt

Wait a minute here I go!!!

AAHHH!

Empty Eyes

Like Van Goh, misunderstood

My thought of you when near I stood

A picture painted perfectly

No one noticed how beautifully

With your presence and your actions

The world ignores, that's their reaction

Like the Mona Lisa, incomplete

Some may say it was meant to be

With no expression on their face

Can't smell the flavor they must taste

You can't tell how they feel

With no emotions, don't know what's real

Empty eyes, can't see no heart

A broken soul been torn apart

Misunderstood, incomplete

A picture perfect masterpiece

A waste of talent for the blind

Hush don't speak or let them shine

Do The Math

My life doesn't change

Because you changed your ways

Because the path you were taking

It's now rearranged

You did the math and I was subtracted

Where I was a plus, I am now just a minus

But my value remains, I am not a remainder

What's left of this equation

Feels somewhat a stranger

I am equal to none or less than, I'm greater

I cannot be figured out by a calculator

My life does not change according to you

According to $1+1=2$

According to your formulas

And your mismatched math

My life does not change

 Nor does my path

Nestle White

Hey there sugar!

You sure are some sweet stuff

Got me going diabetic

Cuz your stuff it's just too much

Come here buttercup

Or should I call you nestle white?

Cuz you sure ain't no dark chocolate

Still your nuts taste OHHH… so right

I love your creamy flavor

I'll eat you by the pound

Like a bag of M & M's

You'll melt right in my mouth

Like a baby with its bottle

You got me so excited

And when I get a craving

Your flavor, it's inviting

Hey there nestle white

You got me bouncing off the walls

And like a sugar rush

I answer to your call

So hey there sweet stuff

Can I get a piece of your creamy nestle white?

If you'll like I'll pay you back with my

Kit kat bar all night

Masked

We're all broken, a little bit bent
A little bit twisted, a little bit spent

None we are perfect, we are all worn
With rips and wrinkles, we are all torn

We all carry burdens, some carry them well
Some we call weak and can easily tell

Some shed their tears and are easily pleased
Other wear a smile too afraid to release

Too afraid to acknowledge
The pain in their skin
Masquerade to the world
With a tornado within

None we are perfect just perfect beliefs

We are all stealing moments, from the next,
we are thieves

We take from each other

 So afraid to give back

We ask for the real

While we wear our own mask

None we are perfect just perfectly fake

Expecting greatness from others

While we're full of mistakes

In A Blink

Time passed so fast

What did I think?

I closed my eyes for a second

Felt like a blink

The years passed me by

Like a movie scene

Like a picture, I see it all

In my mental screen

The characters are us, it is me and my boy

In a world full of struggles

Unfazed by it all while we laid

In our cuddles

When I'm strong enough for him

And I am all that he needs

When he doesn't know any better

And he seems to be pleased

With a blink of the eye time passed us by

And before I knew it

Then came his blue eyes

Friendship was key and he knew about mine

And most important of all

He loved my main prize

So now it's me & my prince

And maybe my King

The questioned that lingered

Until he gifted my ring

Then what felt like a blink

We welcomed our princess

The completion I felt

Not even I could have dreamed this

Then came the roads

And they were too rocky

I thought, I give up

But not even they could have stopped me

So I moved on and fought

For my family and life

And in a blink of the eye

I soon became his wife

So it's me, my princess

My prince and my King

My castle, it's complete

And I wouldn't change a thing

In a blink of the eye

Where did time fly?

My boy is a man

Gone, living his life

I rewind in my mind

Like a movie scene

In a blink of the eye

In my mental screen

Our Song

I don't want you forever

But I need you tonight

If you promise to love me

Even though it's a lie

I'll believe in your lyrics

The sly song you sing

I have no hard feelings

Because it is what it is

I'll believe in your lines

Because you believe in mine

That's how I like it

So honestly full of lies

You come when I call

When I rise, when I fall

And you're gone just as quick

I love the picture you draw

I dance to your songs

Your rhythm your blues

Your lyrics, I've learned them

Sing along to your tunes

I hold on to them

Like I hold on to you

Like I hold on to us

With a grasp that is loose

When you slip through my fingers

I don't hesitate

I don't play the fool

Because I know it's all fake

Then comes tomorrow

And, poof, you are gone

I'll see you when I see you

And this is our song

Moving On

Look at me, I've moved on
Now you're knocking on my door
For so long I wanted you
And it was me you ignored
I cried and begged for your return
My voice you never heard
On my knees, hands on my face
My lesson was well learned

You let me know in your way
To let go and move on
And so I did, I wiped my tears
I was weak, but I grew strong
Now look at me, I've moved on
You're knocking on my door
It's your turn to wipe your tears
And my turn to ignore

Backbone

Where are your shoulders

When I need them to lean on

When my sink is on

And my drain it's clogged

When my eyes are filled

And my heart don't bleed

Where is my soldier

When I'm in need?

Where is my backbone when I can't stand?

Where is your presence to understand?

To wipe me dry when I want to die

To comfort me or at least try

Where are you when you are there?

Close enough to see you do not care

Your physical self looks and see

My soul it's flying, gone mentally

In another world I'm no longer here

Crying and shouting for you to hear

What's inside, what I hold

Volcanos erupting, myself unfolds

When I can't see from blurriness

With one blink I drown from this

And I am here and you are there

Two feet from me with a blank stare

Trapped

Lookee look, I can barely see

My eyes wide open and clear of debris

Still, I am blind to all that is truth

With this house as my shelter

With an invisible roof

With a painted on smile

Make sure to show teeth

With a grin like the joker

Must make THEM believe

Life it's just perfect I just have to breathe

Have self-control and make ME believe

Lookee look, the weight on my chest

I feel like a failure, when I fail all these tests

When I feel I am perfect

And I know I'm a mess

When I can't even control

Or deal with the stress

My eyes are wide open

And I can barely see

What triggers my person

And traps me in me

I feel like a loser with the need to succeed

Searching for the formula

To set my mind free

Misplaced Hatred

Living lonely with so many faces

Misplaced hatred in so many places

Blame myself for what my world's become

Can't think straight stumble with rum

Bad decisions, one after another

So many men, but never a lover

So many moves, so little thoughts

All my gots were all fist fought

So many people, crowded rooms

Bumping into me, well fuck you too

Bad decisions, can't take them back

Burn my bridges in every track

Can't look back, must move ahead

Blame myself for every tear I've shed

Is That Fair To Me?

What is it with me you want in your life?

You have your commitment, ring and your wife

I've asked to let go, it's no longer a game

The feelings I feel are no longer the same

When I lay in my bed, you're in your home

With your wife and your kids, while I lay alone

You've asked me to stay just to love you

Is that fair to me, while you're loving two?

What is it with me that you can't let go?

If it's true you love me, then you let her know

"Until the right time" you've asked me to wait

I need to know now how long will it take?

I need to move on, move on without you

Find me a lover that's loving, and not loving two

A man that is faithful, honest and true

A man that's a man and that man isn't you

Move On And Keep Cruising

Take it as it comes

How do you expect me to feel?

Can't change the situation-----I run

That's how with life I deal

Don't have time to dwell

On something that isn't real

Get out

Pack my bags

My life no one will steal

Can't fix what's unbroken

This I thought you knew

The words were left unspoken

Silly boy-----the sky, it's clearly blue

Move on and keep moving

Take it day by day

Cruise on and keep cruising

A game named life we play

Take a chance

Roll the dice

Some we win and some we lose

The game it's not all nice

So keep on moving as we cruise

Remember Me?

Hello my friend, it's me again

Remember me?

Your worst of enemies

You can't seem to get rid of me

No matter what you try

The pills you pop

The scars you give

Not even all your wine

I'll follow you step by step

No matter where you go

The things you do, you know I know

But I won't tell a soul

Remember me?

Your true best friend

For you I'll do it all

I'll be with you through thick and thin

For you I'll rise and fall

When you are hurt I feel the pain

When you are proud I feel the same

I am all that you have left

Just take a look at yourself

It is me who you reflect

Exhale

I'm on my knees looking up

It is he who I see

He's looking down in my eyes

He can't stop staring at me

He's standing tall, I can see

I have his full attention

I must admit there's no denying

And there's no mistaking

He's standing tall, I'm sitting low

Yet, I'm the one in control

What happens next will he explode?

Will I stay or will I go?

His hands feel good on my head

Massaging my long hair

We're breathing heavy, I'm getting closer

Temptation is truly there

"Before I start, one last thing"

I whisper in his ear

"Point me over in which direction

Do you keep your scuba gear?"

I look at him, he's looking back

I see there's hesitation

He shrugs his shoulders, gives a whisper

"Right now, there's no protection"

I move away, he pulls me closer

To promise a "good time"

With all my strength, I decline

Can't risk my life for one good night

I'm getting dressed, I start to go

Turn to give him one last look

I exhale, I walk away

Another story for my book

Without You

Where do I go from here,

When you're no longer here?

I cannot see your face

Your voice, I cannot hear

What do I do when I need to cry

And you were the one who dried my eyes?

The one who told my truth

The one who never lied

What do I do?

What do I do when I have a choice

When I need to choose

But don't have a voice?

I can't express what I feel inside

When I cannot form my thoughts in lines

When I'm feeling lost and can't be found

When I'm floating off and can't find my
ground

When the thoughts I think are not sound

When you are gone and not around

What do I do?

When I miss your face and a picture won't
do

When I want to visit and talk to you

When I smell your hair in the air

What do I do when you're not there?

When I have a void that can't be filled

When my heart aches till this day, still

When time don't seem to ease this pain

What do I do when it still remains?

I'm Not The Same

Sometimes you grow tired listening to the same song

Repetitious beats, same beat of the drum

Not remembering when this feeling crept up

All you know is you feel it, inside you feel numb

You look at your lover even he's not the same

Nothing has changed he wears the same name

His routine is a rerun his actions don't change

The change is in you, in your heart, in your brain

The beat of this drum, it's beating me insane

It's pounding in me and I smile through the pain

I live in this life and nothing is rearranged

Everyday it's the same, but all out of frame

The pictures are unfocused, unsteady and blurry

Their actions seem joyous, relaxed and unhurried

To me, they are strangers in these frames on my walls

When did I shrink and let everyone get so tall?

Everyone has moved on and I am still here

The beat of this drum is beating my ears

My bottle, it's full and it's filled up with fears

Everything is blurry and my vision's not clear

When did this happen or have I just woken up?

My eyes are wide open, I just want to erupt

Burst out my skin and run to my fame

Nothing has changed, but I'm not the same

To Whom It May Concern

Burning buildings

Crackhead mamas

Farewell fathers

Childhood drama

Lonely souls

Crowded homes

Full of flesh

All alone

Latch key kids

Known as parents

Never given anything

Take nothing for granted

Boarded windows

Unwed moms

Can't find themselves

Can't keep a job

Future fathers

Can't be found

Chasing their manhood

What they believe

Following the footsteps

Of their daddies

Babies having babies

Trying to be grown

Where are their parents

When they're not home?

Single parents

With no degrees

Work two jobs

To make ends meet

America! America!

Turn this around

Educate yourselves

Break new ground

My Bipolar World

I'm standing here going in circles

Uncontrolled spinning with an offbeat tempo

The notes are getting higher and louder by the second

Hands over head, the noise it's deafening

I'm standing here and tears are rolling

I can't explain when I'm not knowing

What's going on inside of me

When I can't breathe controllably

When I can't seem to explain myself

When the bottles no longer decorate the shelves

The medicine cabinet, it's my new fridge

Every meal is like jumping off the bridge

What's wrong with me!?

What's wrong with you!?

Can't you see I'm just confused!?

I'm lost in time

I'm last in line

I'm high, I'm low

What's wrong? I'm fine

I'm standing here going in circles

Too dizzy to see what's luck or miracle

Because I've been gone for so long

Can't tell the difference between right or
wrong

Who to love, who would love me back

With advice I feel attacked

Disconnect myself, I feel laid back

Can't tell the difference between false or
facts

Can't seem to focus on a speeding train

A million miles a minute and it's all the same

Pain & pleasure & love & hate

Good love making or masturbate

All I'm feeling, it's all the same

Pleasure comes around and it still remains

It doesn't change, it refuses to leave

I need the strength to start to release

So thank you & you & you, I see

But I have to find the strength in me

Because I can't be your mission complete

When I am still a mission to me

It Was A Pretty Place

Mommy & Daddy got really sick

And had to go away

They promised to come back for me

When they get better one day

I was put in a foster home

And it was really strange

I was put with strangers

And I was really afraid

Their house, it was so big

 It was a pretty place

They had a fluffy dog

And he would lick my face

He became my best friend

We were the best of buddies

131

We would play so many games

He was very funny

My foster parents would treat me nice

They were very sweet

They would help me with my homework

They would tickle my feet

My foster mom would bake me cookies

My foster dad would blow me bubbles

They would tuck me in for bed

And talk to me when I got in trouble

My foster parents adopted me

And I was very happy

They were now my mom and Dad

We were now a family

One day I noticed

My parent's skin was not the same as mine

I asked my mommy

"Why was my skin a different kind?"

She sat me down and told me a story

How God made many shades

And how inside we are no different

Because we are made the same

I asked my mommy

"Why did I never notice, was it like this all the time?"

She tucked me in, whispered in my ear

"It's because our love is blind"

"She" Lives In Me

I was born a twin

But we are not the same

I like to play pretend

My twin is more the brain

If you look at us

You can't tell us apart

Identical is what they call us

But I am off the charts

If you look and see

I guess twin A's a 10

Then you look at B

And see I am more my friend

I swear we were born triplets

There's "A" & "B" & "she"

No one can really see her
Because "she" lives in me

I like to play pretend
And "she's" my inner me
I feel "she" is my best friend
And my worst of enemies

"She" can't come out and play
"She" lives in secrecy
Sometimes I let her out as "B"
But, "she" is "she", "she" is not me

My mom & dad have met her
They love her very much
To others she must stay inside
We don't want to "make a fuss"

We have so much in common

"She's" who I want to be

Except, the world would notice

Because twin "B" is a he

Dear God

God, I've damned you
I took your name in vain
Yet, when I'm hurt, I turn to you
To help me ease my pain

God, I ask you
Why do you bother with myself?
I don't follow a religion
Don't really care much for my health

God, I thank you
For never letting go
For staying by myside
Knowing the things you know

God, I'm sorry
For all the wrong I've done

I never meant to hurt myself
Never meant to hurt anyone

God, I've damned you
I took your name in vain
But, no matter how I've acted
The love you gave never changed

God, I thank you
For all the strength you've given me
For staying by myside
When I was living selfishly

www.ingramcontent.com/pod-product-compliance
Lightning Source LLC
Chambersburg PA
CBHW031535040426
42445CB00010B/542